THE PONY EXPRESS

Cynthia Mercati

Perfection Learning®

About the Author

Cynthia Mercati is a writer and a professional actress. She has written many plays for a children's theatre that tours and performs at various schools. She also appears in many of the plays herself.

Ms. Mercati loves reading about history and visiting historical places. When she writes a historical play or book, she wants her readers to feel like they are actually living the story.

Ms. Mercati also loves baseball. Her favorite team is the Chicago White Sox. She grew up in Chicago, Illinois, but she now lives in Des Moines, Iowa. Ms. Mercati has two children and one dog.

Cover Illustration: Margaret Sanfilippo
Inside Illustration: Margaret Sanfilippo

Image Credits: St. Joseph Museum, St. Joseph, Missouri/William Hepburn Russell p. 13; Corbis/James Butler Hickok pp. 40, 51; The Denver Public Library, Western History Collection/telegraph wires p. 50

ArtToday (some images copyright www.arttoday.com)

For information, contact
Perfection Learning® Corporation,
1000 North Second Avenue, P.O. Box 500,
Logan, Iowa 51546-0500
Phone: 1-800-831-4190 • Fax: 1-800-543-2745
perfectionlearning.com

ISBN 0-7891-5041-7 Paperback
ISBN 0-7807-9012-x Cover Craft®

1 5 6 7 8 PP 08 07 06 05 04

CONTENTS

INTRODUCTION

Mail delivery was a concern in the New World. Explorers sent messages across the seas. They told about the wonderful land they had discovered to the west. Colonists were always eager for news from Europe. And American settlers wanted to keep in touch with friends and relatives back East.

California was a territory of a few thousand people. Suddenly, after the 1848 Gold Rush, hundreds of thousands of people flocked to the West. And they wanted news about happenings in the East.

At that time, mail only traveled on land as far as St. Joseph, Missouri. Mail to California had to go by ocean around South America.

Then someone came up with a plan to move the mail quickly. And the Pony Express was born.

Charlie Murphy is a Pony Express rider. He is not real. But he is a combination of what every Pony Express rider was. He tells a story that every rider would be proud of.

rode right out onto the boat. It took us to the other side of the river.

The ferry docked. And I **spurred** my horse. We jumped off.

We were in Kansas! We galloped up a hill. Then we sped into the woods. We had many miles to go before reaching the end of our route.

I was a Pony Express rider. The Pony Express carried mail. The route crossed the country from west to east and from east to west.

Pony riders had to cut trails through the mountains. We had to ride through blizzards and blistering heat. We had to fight off outlaws.

But no matter what happened, we could not stop or turn back. The mail had to go through!

Chapter 2

Ships, Stagecoaches, Mules, and Camels

*W*hy was the Pony Express started? People in California wanted their mail faster!

In 1848, California wasn't a state yet. It was a territory. Only about 14,000 Americans lived there.

Then a ranch hand found something.

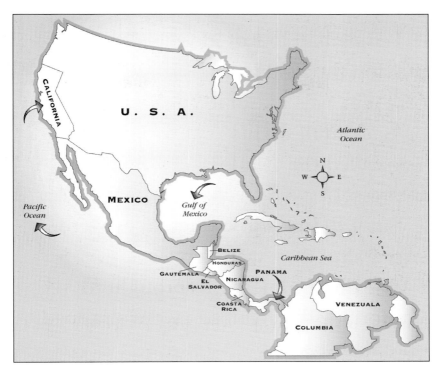

The miners didn't want to wait that long. So the mail was put on steamships. They sailed down the Gulf of Mexico to Panama.

Then the mail went overland to the Pacific Ocean. There another ship carried it to California.

It was faster than the old way. But not fast enough. Mail still took a month to get to the goldfields.

People had lots of ideas about moving the mail west. One idea was to put it on pack mules. This was called the "Mule Express"!

But it didn't work. The mules were strong. But they were too slow.

A team of camels was brought to California! The mailbags were strapped onto their backs.

But the camels were used to walking on soft sand. Now they had to walk on the rocky trails of the West. And their feet got sore!

Next, mail was put on stagecoaches. Four fast horses pulled the coach. A driver sat on top. In case of any trouble, a man sat next to the driver. He had a shotgun.

Six passengers sat inside. Three mail sacks were packed on top.

But the stagecoaches were too slow. It took them 25 days.

"There has to be another way," the lonely miners said.

But what? They had tried ships, stagecoaches, mules, and camels. Everything had failed!

Then a man named William Hepburn Russell came up with a plan.

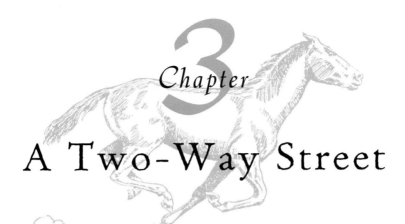

Chapter 3

A Two-Way Street

The idea was to hire young men. They would ride fast horses to carry the mail!

Mail came to St. Joseph from the East. It traveled by train.

Riders would pick up mail in St. Joseph. Then they would carry it to Sacramento. Riders from Sacramento would ride the other way. They would carry mail to St. Joseph.

Russell named this system the Pony Express.

He mapped out a trail. It would cover 1,800 miles. Along that trail, he would build about 190 **relay stations**.

They would be 5 to 20 miles apart. They would have just one room.

A station keeper and his helper would live in each station. Their job would be simple. They would have a fresh horse ready when a rider came through.

Home stations would be built. They would be 75 miles apart.

A Pony Express rider would pick up mail at his home station. Then he would ride as fast as his horse could go. At each relay station, he would change to a fresh

horse. He would ride until he came to the next home station. Then the rider would hand the mail to the next rider.

The arriving rider would rest and eat. He would wait for another rider to come. That rider would bring mail from the other way.

When the second rider arrived, the first rider would grab the mail sack. Then he would gallop 75 miles back to the home station he had started from.

A letter would cost five dollars per half an ounce. That was a lot of money! But it only would take *ten* days to get to California.

The Pony Express would become a two-way street. It would link both ends of the country!

Chapter 4

Horses and Mailbags

$\mathcal{T}$he Pony Express needed 500 horses! The eastern end of the route was all flat plains and prairies. It was like a racetrack! So racing horses were bought for that part of the ride. They were called **thoroughbreds**. They were sleek and fast.

The western end of the route had mountains and deserts. **Mustangs** were needed for that part. They were tough and strong. But they couldn't be bought.

Mustangs roamed free on the range. They had to be rounded up.

All the horses were small. Small horses could cover more ground than big horses. And they were quicker.

But small horses couldn't carry much weight. So special saddles were made for the riders. They weighed only a third as much as regular saddles.

A special kind of saddlebag was made too. It was called a *mochila*.

The *mochila* was a square leather blanket. It had four hard leather pockets. One was sewn on each corner. These were called **cantinas**. The *mochila* fit over the saddle. Two of the *cantinas* were in front of the rider. Two were behind him.

Mail was wrapped in oiled silk. This protected the mail from the weather. Then it was locked in the pockets. The pockets weren't opened until the mail reached its delivery point.

The rider sat on the *mochila*. Then it couldn't be lost or stolen while the rider was on his horse.

Finally, the stations were built. The horses were bought and rounded up. The saddles were made. And the mailbags were finished. Everything was ready for the Pony Express. All was ready except one thing. They needed riders! That's where I came in!

Chapter 5

A Need for Adventure

I had read about the Pony Express in the newspaper. I told my brother about it. I thought it was a good idea.

"This is a fast-moving country," I said. "Americans are in a hurry all the time. They want their mail

fast too! I wish I could be part of the Pony Express!"

This was my chance!

I had everything they were looking for. I was young. I was just 17 years old. And I was skinny!

I had grown up on a farm in Missouri. My job had been to train the horses. I had ridden in lots of races too. I had won most of them!

The only family I had was my brother. I told him I was going to apply for the job.

"I think you would make a good rider, Charlie," he said. "But it sounds too dangerous. That's why they don't want men with families. They don't want your family to be sad if you die. The ad even says you have to be ready to risk your life!"

"I know it will be dangerous," I answered. "But that's what I want. Farm life is too tame for me.

"After Ma and Pa died, I stayed on to help you with the work. But now you have hired another man. You don't need me. I'm ready for some adventure!"

"Then I hope the Pony Express picks you to be one of their riders," Tom said. He clapped me on the back. "Good luck!"

———◆►◄◆◄———

Our farm wasn't very far away from St. Joseph. It only took one day on the stagecoach.

There were lots of other young men at the Overland Express Building. In fact, there were hundreds of them! And all of them wanted to be Pony Express riders!

Some had come from farms, like me. Some had come from ranches or mining camps. Others had been fur trappers or scouts for the army. One had even been a schoolteacher.

Only 80 men were chosen. I was proud to be one of them!

Chapter 6

Irish Charlie

*A*ll Pony Express riders had to promise three things.

1. We would not drink liquor.
2. We would not use bad language.
3. We would not pick fights with other riders.

And if we ever harmed a horse, we would be fired.

We were paid $25.00 a week. That was a lot of money! Between rides we lived for free at the home stations. We also got our meals free.

Mostly we ate dried meat and beans. Sometimes a stationmaster hired a hunter to shoot some game. Then we had fresh meat. And there was always freshly baked bread waiting for us.

Each rider got a revolver, a shotgun, and a Bible. We had to carry them with us on our rides.

The guns were for protection. Sometimes riders were attacked by animals, like bears or wolves. Or they might be **ambushed** by bandits.

But after a while, some riders didn't carry the guns. They added too much weight. The riders depended only on the speed of their horses.

The river had overflowed its banks. Upson rode his horse upstream. He found a safe spot to cross. At least, he thought it was safe.

Suddenly, the pony's head disappeared in a **geyser**! It had been hidden under the river's surface.

Upson grabbed the *mochila* and held it over his head. He urged his pony on.

They finally reached the other side. Boston was soaked. But the mail was dry.

Heavy snow started to fall. Upson dismounted. He continued on foot. He led his pony.

He had to **break a trail** as they went. In some places, snowdrifts were 20 feet high!

Upson lost his way. He and his pony fell down into a gorge.

Horse and rider tumbled into a stand of trees.

Upson got up and remounted. He took off again. Finally he reached the end of his route.

Upson had ridden 55 miles across the highest part of the mountains during a terrible snowstorm. And he had done it in just 8 hours!

———◆◆✕◆◆———

Once, a rider named Billie Campbell was riding west. Suddenly he heard the sound of hooves. There must have been thousands of hooves!

He looked around. A buffalo herd was thundering straight for him!

Quickly, Billie pulled on the reins. He turned the horse. With only inches to spare, they rode out of the way of the stampeding buffalo!

Some riders had to cross a hot desert. It stretched across Nevada and into Utah.

Not one blade of grass grew on that trail. Instead, the sandy soil blew up thick, choking dust.

Often I got very tired on my run. Sometimes I even fell asleep right in the saddle. That happened to lots of riders. But our ponies worked just as hard as we did.

———◆▸✦◂◆———

Once, a rider was killed in the saddle. He fell to the ground.

The riderless horse did not stop. He galloped on to deliver the mail pouch to the next station!

———◆▸✦◂◆———

There was a jet-black horse. His name was Black Billy. And he was a real hero.

His rider was attacked. American Indians shot two arrows into Black Billy's flanks.

But the horse kept on. He didn't stop until he reached the next station.

Black Billy had wanted the mail to go through just as much as his rider had!

Chapter 9

Doughnuts and Famous Riders

It's because of the Pony Express that doughnuts were invented!

Johnny Fry was a rider. He had a girlfriend who baked sweet biscuits. She would stand by the trail. As he rode by, she passed him the biscuits.

But Johnny had trouble. He couldn't hold the reins and the biscuits at the same time.

So Johnny's girlfriend baked her biscuits with a hole in the middle. Johnny could spear the biscuits with one finger and still keep both hands on the reins! And so the doughnut as we know it was born!

James Butler Hickok worked for the

Pony Express. He was at the Rock Creek Station. He took care of the horses.

One day, four outlaws rode up to the station. They were the McCanles gang.

They had told people they were going to make trouble for the Pony Express. The stationmaster was very frightened. So Hickok went outside. Alone, he faced the outlaws.

There was a shoot-out. Hickok won! After that, Rock Creek Station had no more trouble from the McCanles gang.

Hickok later became known as "Wild Bill" Hickok!

Bill Cody was one of the youngest Pony Express riders. He was only 15. He took the job to support his mother and sisters.

Once, Bill Cody heard a rumor. Some outlaws were waiting for him along the trail. They had heard that Bill was carrying a special box in his mailbag. The box was full of money.

But Bill had a plan. He packed an empty *mochila*. He stuffed the four *cantinas* with paper.

He hadn't gone very far when the two outlaws ambushed him. The outlaws saw how young Bill was. They howled with laughter. He was going to be easy "pickin's"!

Bill said he would give them the mailbag. Then he took out the fake *mochila*.

Quick as a flash, he threw it at one of the men. The *mochila* knocked the outlaw out of his saddle.

Next, Bill shot the other outlaw in the arm. With the real mailbag safe, Bill took off lickety-split down the trail!

Bill Cody might be someone you've heard of. He became known as "Buffalo Bill" Cody!

Chapter 10

The Indian War

Many men went west to hunt for gold. But they treated the Indians badly. They took over the Indians' land. They killed their game. They polluted the rivers and streams.

Many tribes were very angry. The **Paiute** became so angry they declared war on all white settlements on their land.

Many of these settlements were Pony Express stations.

The Paiute began burning the stations. They drove off the horses. They killed the stationmasters and their helpers.

Soon, the Sioux, Cheyenne, Shoshone, and Arapaho declared war on the Pony Express too.

We were told not to shoot at the Indians. We were to outrun them.

Our horses were faster than theirs. This was because Indian horses ate only grass. Our horses ate only grain. Grain-fed horses could run faster than grass-fed horses.

Buffalo Bill Cody was attacked by Paiute on one of his rides. He lay down flat on his horse's neck. He dug in his spurs. Sure enough, his pony soon outran the Indian ponies.

Once, I found the trail blocked by a large group of Indians. They were all armed. They stared at me. I stared at them. It was too late to turn my horse and try to outrun them.

Slowly I drew my revolver. I threw it on the ground. I did the same with my shotgun.

Then I rode my horse right up to them. I lifted my hand. And I made the peace sign.

Their leader raised his hand. He returned the sign. Then he motioned for me to go on my way.

During the Indian War, Pony Bob Haslam set a record for riders.

He had made his regular run. And he was back at his home station. But the next rider wouldn't take the mail. He was too scared! So Pony Bob got on the fresh horse himself.

He found the next relay station in flames. The stationmaster was dead.

So Pony Bob rode on. And he rode on! Finally, he got to the next home station. He was far away from his own home station.

But Pony Bob had made it! He handed over the mail. He had covered 384 miles in 36 hours!

That was the longest ride in Pony Express history.

Longest Ride

Pony Bob Haslam did make the longest ride in Pony Express history. But he stopped for a break. He slept for nine hours at Smith's Creek before continuing west.

Buffalo Bill Cody is credited with making the longest nonstop ride.

The distance for both men's rides is not certain. Both have been listed as riding 384 miles. And both have been listed as riding fewer miles.

But one thing's for sure. Both men were dedicated to delivering the mail.

The Indian War forced the Pony Express to stop for three weeks. People missed their letters! So they complained to the government.

The cavalry was sent in to protect the riders. This ended the Indian uprising. Once again, the mail went through!

Chapter 11

The End of the Trail

Abraham Lincoln was elected President of the United States in 1860.

The news was telegraphed from Washington D.C. to St. Joseph to Fort Kearney, Nebraska. The Pony Express took the news the rest of the way to California.

But by July 1861, men were stringing telegraph wires all across the West. By October, the last link in the telegraph line was finished. Now news could be wired from coast to coast in a moment.

The Pony Express was no longer needed. It came to an end in October. What happened to some of the riders?

Buffalo Bill worked as a scout for the army. He was hired by the railroad. He hunted buffalo to feed the railroad crews.

Later, he started "Buffalo Bill's Wild West Show." It toured all over the United States and Europe. One of the most popular acts showed a Pony rider changing horses at a relay station!

Wild Bill Hickok became the mayor of Abilene, Kansas. The people wanted Wild Bill to bring law and order to their town.

Johnny Fry—of doughnut fame— joined the Union army in the Civil War.

Pony Bob Haslam rode for the Wells Fargo stagecoach. Then he became a deputy marshal.

I went to work for the army. I trained horses for the cavalry. As long as I was around horses, I was happy!

The Pony Express was only in business for 18 months. During that short time, it delivered more than 30,000 pieces of mail. Only one mailbag was ever lost!

The telegraph, and all that came later, were faster than the Pony Express. That's for sure. But they weren't as exciting!

People talked about the Pony Express for many years. They told stories about the famous riders. They even wrote books about it—like this one!

Some people even say that on a clear night, if you look hard enough, you can still see a Pony Express rider galloping down the old trail. And if you listen hard enough, you can hear the echo of the wild Coyote Yell!

GLOSSARY

ambush to attack someone by surprise

break a trail make a new path

buckskin soft leather made from deerskin

cantinas four pockets on the *mochila*, used to carry the mail; from the Spanish language

ferry boat to carry people and things across a body of water

flank side of a horse

geyser underground spring that sends up heated water and steam

gorge   narrow passage through land

home station   place where the Pony Express riders started and ended their rides; place where they rested and ate between rides.

migration   movement from one place to another

mochila   special saddlebag to carry mail; from the Spanish language

mustang   small, hardy horse that roamed the western prairies

Paiute	American Indian tribe that lived in Utah, Arizona, Nevada, and California
relay station	place where the Pony Express riders changed horses
spur	to urge forward
stable	place where horses are kept
thoroughbred	breed of light, speedy horses used for racing